The Monroe Doctrine

An End to European Colonies in America

Magdalena Alagna

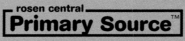

rosen central
Primary Source™
The Rosen Publishing Group, Inc., New York

Published in 2004 by The Rosen Publishing Group, Inc.
29 East 21st Street, New York, NY 10010

Library of Congress Cataloging-in-Publication Data

Alagna, Magdalena.
The Monroe Doctrine: an end to European colonies in America / by Magdalena Alagna.— 1st ed.
    p. cm. — (Life in the new American nation)
Summary: Explores the history of the Monroe Doctrine, which grew from President Monroe's 1823 speech to Congress into a lasting policy on how the United States should behave toward European nations.
Includes bibliographical references (p.) and index.
ISBN 0-8239-4040-3 (lib. bdg.)
ISBN 0-8239-4258-9 (pbk. bdg.)
6-pack ISBN 0-8239-4271-6
1. Monroe doctrine—Juvenile literature. 2. United States—Foreign relations—Europe—Juvenile literature. 3. Europe—Foreign relations—United States—Juvenile literature.
4. International cooperation—Juvenile literature. [1. Monroe doctrine. 2. United States—Foreign relations—Europe. 3. Europe—Foreign relations—United States. 4. International relations.] I. Title. II. Series.
JZ1482.A42 2003
327.7304—dc21

2002156104

Manufactured in the United States of America

Cover image (left side): The Monroe Doctrine
Cover image (right side): 1912 painting by Clyde De Land of the birth of the Monroe Doctrine (Left to right): John Irving Adams, William Harris Crawford, William Wirt, President James Monroe, John Caldwell Calhoun, Daniel D. Tompkins, and John McLean

Photo credits: cover photos (left), p. 14 © The National Archives and Records Administration; cover photos (right), p. 1 © Bettmann/Corbis; pp. 5, 12, 16, 22, 24, 26 © Library of Congress; pp. 7, 19, 20, 25 © Hulton/Archive/Getty Images; p. 10 © Corbis.

Designer: Nelson Sá; Editor: Eliza Berkowitz; Photo Researcher: Nelson Sá

Contents

Introduction

The Monroe Doctrine is a policy, or course of action. This policy explains how the United States should behave toward European nations. It is called the Monroe Doctrine because it originated with President James Monroe. There are four parts to the Monroe Doctrine.

The first part states that European nations cannot consider any part of North America as a good place for a colony. The second part states that the nations in the Western Hemisphere are different from those in Europe. They are different because they were republics and not monarchies. A republic is a form of government in which the authority belongs to the people. In a monarchy, a king or queen runs the government. The third part states that no European nation can make an independent state in the Western Hemisphere do things the way the European nation wants them to be done. By saying that, Monroe made

America the protector of independent nations in the Western Hemisphere. The last part of the Monroe Doctrine states that America will not get in the middle of any European matters.

What made President Monroe give this message to Congress in 1823? Certain events in Europe happening at that time made Americans nervous. Americans

This portrait of James Monroe was painted by Charles Bird King and engraved by Goodman & Piggot. It was created in 1817. Monroe, the fifth president of the United States, is pictured in the White House with a view of the Capitol. The Monroe Doctrine bears Monroe's name because it was based on some of his political ideas.

worried that North American nations could not stay independent from Europe. One concern was that Spain wanted to get back its North American colonies. Certain nations in Europe wanted to help Spain do this. These nations were called the Holy Alliance. They would help by sending soldiers to fight in the colonies. These colonies had recently won their independence from Spain. The colonies had fought hard to gain their independence. They did not want to be forced to fight again to keep their freedom.

On August 16, 1823, George Canning, a British official, talked with Richard Rush. Rush was the official who represented the United States in London. The British government did not think it was right that French soldiers had fought in Spain. The British also thought that France and the Holy Alliance should not send soldiers to Latin America. Canning told Rush that he thought Britain and the United States should be allies, or friends. This might sound like a good idea. However, if America and Britain became allies, that would change how

Europe thought of the United States. Europe might not see America as a strong nation that could stand up for itself.

Monroe and his advisers also had two other concerns about Europe. The first concern was that Russia had shown that it might want to have colonies in North America. Russian ruler Alexander I gave an

George Canning, a British politician, is pictured here greeting a crowd from the window of a building in England in 1812. Canning later met with Richard Rush to discuss concerns about Latin America. Their talks led to the Monroe Doctrine.

order that closed the waters off Alaska to ships of other nations. This action made the United States think that Russia wanted colonies in North America.

The second concern was whether to recognize Greece as a nation officially. At that time, Greece was not considered a country. No European state had recognized Greece yet. President Monroe had to decide whether the United States should be the first country to recognize Greece officially. If the United States did that, they would be taking the lead in a European matter. The United States wanted Europe to stay out of American affairs. It might not be a good idea for America to become involved in European affairs.

History of the Monroe Doctrine

The issues facing President Monroe during his presidency in the early nineteenth century were not new. In the seventeenth century, many Englishmen in the Americas thought the American colonies should be involved in Britain's affairs. Others believed that the colonies should stay out of Britain's affairs. Then in the eighteenth century, Britain and France fought a series of wars that resulted in the Seven Years' War (1756–1763). Again, some colonists thought America should get involved. Others thought America should stay out of the European conflict.

Many colonists felt that the British in America were different from the British subjects who were in Britain. Were the British in America faithful to

Décoration du Feu d'Artifice tiré à Londres en Réjouissance de la Paix en 1763.

This is a print of a fireworks display to celebrate the end of the Seven Years' War. There was much discussion in America about whether the United States should get involved in the Seven Years' War. The country was still figuring out how it would handle foreign conflicts.

America or to Britain? No one knew for sure. It was a time of deep political uncertainty in America. Some people were more faithful to Britain. There were others who wanted to see America be independent of Britain.

This wish for independence was one of the feelings that led to the American Revolution. During the American Revolution, the Continental Congress said that the United States should not get involved in European politics. America wanted to be free of Britain, a European power. Many people thought America should keep itself separate from European politics. It sounds simple, but it was not that easy. The United States needed to make an ally of France. France helped America to win its independence from Britain. Also, the United States needed to keep trading with the nations of Europe. War costs a lot of money. American colonies needed the money from trade with European nations to fight for their freedom from Britain.

America eventually won its independence from Britain. Questions arose about how to behave toward European nations. President George Washington, the first president in the new nation, was very worried about the question of America's involvement in European politics.

President Monroe and his advisers were asking complex questions in 1823. Was the United States part of the European political system? Was there a different set

Washington's Speech

In 1796, President George Washington made the most famous of many speeches against making European allies. He stated, "[H]istory and experience prove that foreign influence is one of the most baneful foes of republican government." In short, Washington did not believe the United States should be allied with European nations.

This is a portrait of George Washington, the first president of the United States. During Washington's presidency, he questioned how the new nation should deal with many issues. European matters were a big concern at the time. Such questions continued into James Monroe's presidency and beyond.

of politics for North America? The United States had been dealing with these questions for a long time before Monroe became president.

In 1823, no one thought President Monroe had done anything important in giving his message to Congress. It was a long time before anyone realized the impact of his speech. No one thought that the effects of the Monroe Doctrine would be long lasting. They did not think the Monroe Doctrine could be applied to situations other than the one with Spain in 1823.

Domestic Concerns Chapter 2

The Monroe Doctrine sounds simple on paper. However, many different concerns went into the making of the Monroe Doctrine. In 1824, there was a presidential election. Monroe planned to retire. Many felt that the secretary of state, John Quincy Adams, would be the next president. In fact, Adams wanted to run for president. His victory would depend on how the United States behaved toward European nations at this time.

The Republican Party was the leading political party at that time. If Adams wanted to be president, he needed a large number of Republicans to vote for him. Not everyone wanted Adams to be president. Some of his enemies remembered that his father,

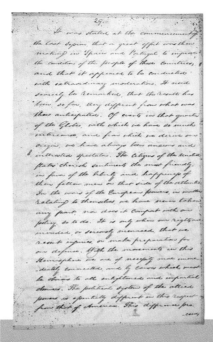
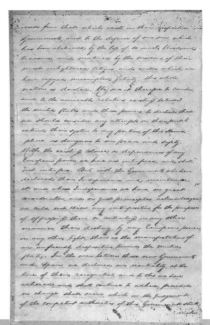

This is a copy of the Monroe Doctrine. At the time that the Monroe Doctrine was created, no one knew that it would influence politics in the future. However, it affected foreign policy into the twentieth century.

John Adams, had been a Federalist. They also knew that the son had been a Federalist until 1808.

One difference between Republicans and Federalists had to do with how they felt America should act toward Britain. The Federalists wanted good relations with the British. If Monroe decided that the United States should be an ally with Britain, many Americans would think Adams had made Monroe decide that. This is because Adams was a Federalist. They would say that Adams was still a Federalist who wanted good relations with Britain. Then no one in the Republican Party would vote for him. If America recognized Greece as an official country, that would also make Adams look like a Federalist. This is because most of the people who wanted to recognize Greece were Federalists.

Secretary of War John C. Calhoun also was running for president. He thought the United States should be Britain's ally. He also thought America should recognize Greece. Past presidents Thomas Jefferson and James Madison also thought America should ally with Britain and recognize Greece. Both of these men did not want John Quincy Adams to be elected president. Calhoun,

Jefferson, and Madison were important men. President Monroe would listen to them. John Quincy Adams had to take strong action if he wanted to have a chance at being elected president.

The first thing Adams did was to tell Monroe that there was only a small chance that Europe would interfere in Latin America. If Britain decided to take

John Quincy Adams was the sixth president of the United States. This portrait of Adams was painted by Thomas Sully in 1826. Adams had many ideas on how the United States should behave toward European nations. His ideas became the main points of the Monroe Doctrine, which influenced America's dealings with other nations for years to come.

action in Latin America, it would do so because it wanted to. It wouldn't matter much to Britain if America were an ally in the business. Basically, Adams told Monroe to act independently of Britain. Then if the British wanted to do what the Americans were doing, they would.

Adams also told Monroe his views on the Greece issue. He said the United States should not recognize Greece as a nation. Adams said that America should continue to act in a way that kept it separate from the politics of Europe. What Adams said to Monroe is basically what later became the Monroe Doctrine. The Monroe Doctrine was written mostly from the ideas of John Quincy Adams.

Monroe thought Adams was right. Monroe told Adams to tell the Russian official in Washington that the United States would oppose Russia's move to make colonies in the Americas. The United States would also oppose any move by the Holy Alliance to help Spain get back its American colonies.

Chapter 3   The Doctrine After 1823

At first, even the U.S. government did not see how the Monroe Doctrine could be used in foreign policy. The United States did not want Europe to interfere in Latin America. However, the United States did not seem eager to make Latin American friends. In 1826, Panama wanted the United States as an ally. The United States said no. The foreign policy of the United States seemed to be one of not drawing attention to itself. The country did not make enemies, but it did not make friends, either.

The policy of the United States concerning Latin America firmed up over the years. Many times in the 1850s, the United States warned European nations to stay out of its dealings with

DECEMBER 17, 1902.]

PUNCH, OR THE LONDON CHARIVARI.

117

CORNERING HIM.

Little Venezuela. "YAH! YOU BIG BULLIES! YOU DAREN'T GIT OVER THAT FENCE!"
England and Germany (together). "ALL RIGHT, YOUNG MAN, WE CAN WAIT!"

This cartoon, published in 1902, represents England and Germany responding to the Venezuelan blockage at the end of the nineteenth century. The Monroe Doctrine was useful in this situation because it forced European powers to keep away from affairs in the Western Hemisphere.

Mexico. This may have started in the late 1840s when President James K. Polk warned Britain and France not to interfere in the fight that the United States had with Mexico. This fight would become the Mexican War (1846–1848). On April 29, 1848, Polk gave a message to England and Spain. The message stated that an English or Spanish action over Yucatán would go against the Monroe Doctrine of 1823. Polk warned

This is a print of a battle at Palo Alto during the Mexican War. During the late 1840s, the United States began arguing with Mexico. This fighting eventually became the Mexican War, in which European forces wanted to get involved. The Monroe Doctrine, however, prevented that from happening.

that the threat of this action might make the United States take control over Yucatán. This message was the first time that the Monroe Doctrine was used to show the world that the United States could obtain more territory. No action was taken, however.

Americans didn't always use the Monroe Doctrine when dealing with Europe. In the 1860s, the U.S. government did not say anything outright about the Monroe Doctrine when protesting Spain's action in the Dominican Republic. However, some members of Congress said that the U.S. was using the Monroe Doctrine. The Dominican Republic became independent in 1865. This seemed to show that the Monroe Doctrine was being respected by Europe.

Use of the Monroe Doctrine continued into the 1870s and the 1880s. At the end of the nineteenth century, President Grover Cleveland used the Monroe Doctrine. He demanded that Britain talk with Venezuela about the boundary between Venezuela and Guiana, a British colony in Latin America. Great Britain might have been happy to push the boundary of its colony into Venezuela without talking to anyone about it first. However, President Cleveland's saying that Britain had to talk to Venezuela sent a clear message. The message was that Britain could not do whatever it wanted in Latin America. If it did, it would have to answer to the

Building Canals

President Ulysses S. Grant used the Monroe Doctrine when Europeans wanted to build canals for trade in North America. Grant made certain that the United States had a voice in how these canals were built. But Great Britain was not happy about this. However, in the 1880s, the United States and Great Britain finally agreed about the issue. It became the first Hay-Pauncefote Treaty, on February 5, 1900.

This map of South America was created in 1826. South America is the southern portion of the Western Hemisphere. The Monroe Doctrine prevented European nations from interfering in matters of the Western Hemisphere, although the United States was still able to be involved in such matters.

United States. Britain backed down, showing that the Monroe Doctrine worked in keeping the Western Hemisphere separate from the politics of Europe.

The Doctrine in the Modern Age

After World War I, countries in Latin America began to dislike the Monroe Doctrine. Latin American republics were not excited about having the United States involved in their governments. The United States came to be seen as an older brother or sister who could either be helpful or bullying, depending on your point of view. Americans made new policies to keep up with the changing views about the Monroe Doctrine.

President Franklin D. Roosevelt said that the United States would not do armed interventions. That means doing interventions with soldiers and weapons. Roosevelt made this statement at the seventh Pan-American Conference in 1933. He signed

This is a portrait of President Franklin Delano Roosevelt from 1933. Roosevelt was president from 1933 to 1945. He was the only president to have been elected for four terms of presidency. Roosevelt was the first president to stop armed interventions in Latin American countries by signing a treaty in 1933.

a treaty with several Latin American countries. They all agreed not to interfere in the affairs of one another.

The rest of the world has never officially recognized the Monroe Doctrine. President Woodrow Wilson had to talk about the Monroe Doctrine because of the World War I peace talks in 1919. There were people in the United States who did not want to be in the League of Nations. They feared it would go against the Monroe Doctrine. Wilson added an article to the peace treaty. It said that nothing in the peace treaty could go against an

In 1919, the major world powers formed the Treaty of Versailles. The treaty was meant to ensure a lasting peace. In this picture, Prime Minister David Lloyd George of Great Britain (*left*), Prime Minister Georges Clemenceau of France (*middle*), and U.S. President Woodrow Wilson (*right*) head to the Versailles Peace Conference.

understanding like the Monroe Doctrine. Even that article didn't set all Americans' fears at rest.

Does that article being included in such an important treaty mean that Europe recognizes the Monroe Doctrine? Not exactly. There are even some Americans who wonder if the Monroe Doctrine is a good idea. Many documents were written about the Monroe Doctrine whenever the United States wanted to make treaties with other countries. For instance, the U.S. Senate considered a document called the

Kellogg-Briand Pact of 1929. It is also called the Pact of Paris. The pact stated that the United States would try peaceful ways of settling international conflict. Congress added a separate report that dealt with the Monroe Doctrine.

In 1948, the Organization of American States was established. Its ideas went into effect in December 1951. Many of its ideas were about using the Monroe

This photograph was taken in 1929 during a ceremony at the White House to celebrate the signing of the Kellogg-Briand Pact. For the United States, this pact meant that it would attempt peaceful ways of settling conflicts with other nations.

Doctrine throughout all of the Western Hemisphere. North and South American (and Caribbean) countries standing together in thought, feeling, and action is called Pan-Americanism. Pan-Americanism was put to the test by the United States's fear of communist activity in Latin America. The United States took action in Guatemala in 1954, in Cuba from 1960 to 1961, and in the Dominican Republic in 1965. The United States took this action without considering how the other North American countries would feel. Generally, the United States wants to support Pan-Americanism.

The Monroe Doctrine was very useful in 1823, when the United States wanted to make itself separate from the politics of Europe. The doctrine has not always been as useful in U.S. foreign policy. Sometimes other nations wanted America to mind its own business. Other times, the Monroe Doctrine has led America into a larger idea of what being American is.

Glossary

article (AR-tih-kul) A piece of writing that adds a new idea to a law that already exists.

campaign (kam-PAYN) A plan to obtain a certain result, such as to win an election.

communist (KAH-myoo-nist) Having to do with a political party that believes goods should be owned by the state and shared by all people in the state.

conference (KON-frints) A meeting.

Congress (KON-gres) The part of the U.S. government that makes laws.

Continental Congress (kon-tin-EN-tul KON-gres) A group, made up of a few people from every colony, that made decisions for the colonies.

defense (dih-FENS) Having to do with sticking up for yourself or protecting yourself.

foreign policy (FOR-in PAH-lih-see) A way of behaving with all the world's nations.

interfere (in-ter-FEER) To take action where none is wanted.

intervention (in-ter-VEN-shun) To take action to help solve a problem between two parties.

monarchy (MAH-nar-kee) A government run by a king or queen.

organize (OR-guh-nyz) To arrange.

presidential election (preh-sih-DEN-shul ee-LEK-shun) Choosing someone to be president by voting for him or her.

republic (ree-PUB-lik) A form of government in which the authority belongs to the people.

Republicans (rih-PUB-lih-kens) People belonging to a party that believes government power should rest with those people who are chosen by citizens.

revolution (reh-vuh-LOO-shun) A complete change in government.

Senate (SEH-nit) A law-making part of the U.S. government.

threat (THRET) Something that can cause harm.

Western Hemisphere (WES-tern HEH-mih-sfeer) The half of the world that includes North America and South America.

Web Sites

Due to the changing nature of Internet links, the Rosen Publishing Group, Inc., has developed an online list of Web sites related to the subject of this book. This site is updated regularly. Please use this link to access the list:

http://www.rosenlinks.com/lnan/modo

Primary Source Image List

Page 1: Drawing by T. A. Rogue. Created on December 16, 1902.
Page 5: Stipple engraving, painted by Charles Bird King and engraved by Goodman & Piggot. Created on December 15, 1817.
Page 10: Color print created in 1763. Housed in Archivo Iconografico in San Antonio.
Page 12: Portrait by Gilbert Stuart. Created in 1796. Housed at the Museum of the City of New York.
Page 14: Monroe Doctrine created in 1823. Housed in the National Archives and Records Administration building in Washington, DC.
Page 16: Engraving by Asher Brown Durand from a painting by Thomas Sully. Created on October 6, 1826.
Page 19: Print by Bernard Partridge. Created on December 17, 1902.
Page 20: Color print by Nathaniel Currier. Created on May 8, 1846.
Page 22: Map by Anthony Finely. Created in 1826. Housed at the Library of Congress, Geography and Map Division.
Page 24: Photograph taken in 1935. Housed at the National Photo Company Collection in Washington, DC.
Page 26: Photograph taken on July 24, 1929. Housed at the National Photo Company Collection in Washington, DC.

Index

About the Author

Magdalena Alagna is a writer and editor living in New York City.